DOT1Q PUBLISHING

The Legislative Process

Enactment of a Law, Volume 2

Robert B. Dove
Parliamentarian, United States Senate
1/19/2010

Published by dot1q Publishing
Copyright © by dot1q Publishing
Cover Copyright © by dot1q Publishing

ISBN: 978-0-9826266-1-0

First Printing 2010
Printed in the United States of America

TABLE OF CONTENTS

This page was intentionally left blank.

1

INTRODUCTION

The legislative branch of government has responsibilities which in many cases transcend the process of enactment of legislation. Among these are the Senate's power of advice and consent with regard to treaties and nominations. The preeminent role of the legislative branch, however, is its concern with legislation.

"All legislative Powers" granted to the Federal government by the Constitution, as stated in Article I, Section I, are vested in a Congress of the United States, which shall consist of a Senate and House of Representatives. The Congress meets at least once a year and has been doing so since 1789 in the following locations: from March 4, 1789 through August 12, 1790, in Federal Hall, New York, New York; from December 6, 1790 through December 2, 1799, in Congress Hall, Philadelphia, Pennsylvania; and from November 17, 1800, at the Capitol, in Washington, D. C.

Since the Constitution prescribes that there be two Senators from each State, the Senate is presently composed of 100 Members. Also pursuant to the Constitution, a Senator must be at least 30 years of age, have been a citizen of the United States for nine years, and, when elected, be a resident of the State for which the Senator is chosen. The term of office is six years and approximately one-third of the total membership of the Senate is elected every second year.

2

CONTRASTING PROCEDURES OF THE SENATE AND THE HOUSE

The order of business in the Senate is simpler than that of the House. While the procedure of both bodies is basically founded on Jefferson's Manual of Parliamentary Practice, the practices of the two bodies are at considerable variance. The order and privileged status of motions and the amending procedure of the two are at less variance than their method of calling up business. The business of the Senate (bills and resolutions) is not divided into classes as a basis for their consideration, nor are there calendar days set aside each month in the Senate for the consideration of particular bills and resolutions. The nature of bills has no effect on the order or time of their initial consideration.

The Senate, like the House, gives certain motions a privileged status over others and certain business, such as conference reports, command first or immediate consideration, under the theory that a bill which has reached the conference stage has been moved a long way toward enactment and should be privileged when compared with bills that have only been reported.

At any time the Presiding Officer may lay, or a Senator may move to lay, before the Senate any bill or other matter sent to the Senate by the President or the House of Representatives, and any pending question or business at that time shall be suspended, but not displaced. Included in this category are veto messages, which constitute privileged business and which may be brought up at almost any time; however, a Senator cannot be deprived of his right to the floor for this purpose nor may certain business be interrupted, such as approving the Journal, while the Senate is dividing "or while a question of order or a motion to adjourn is pending."

The Senate is a continuing body as contrasted with the House. Two-thirds of the Senators of an old Congress return to the subsequent new one without having to be re-elected, but all Representatives must stand for re-election every two years. Thus the manner and extent of organizing each new Senate have not been established under the influence of definite breaks between each Congress as has been the experience of the House, nor have the parliamentary rules of the Senate been equally subjected to alterations. Representatives re-adopt their old rules of procedure at the inception of each Congress, often with slight modification, while Senators have not given a general reaffirmation to their rules since 1789. The rules adopted by the Senate in the first Congresses have remained in force continuously, with the exceptions of particular additions or abolishments from time to time. Any such changes are made by amending the rules to meet new needs of the body. Changes have not been frequent, as demonstrated by the fact that a codification of the accumulated alterations has occurred on only a few different occasions.

The continuity of sessions of the same Congress is provided for by the Senate rules:

At the second or any subsequent session of a Congress, the legislative business of the Senate which remained undetermined at the close of the next preceding session of that Congress shall be resumed and proceeded with in the same manner as if no adjournment of the Senate had taken place. (Rule XVIII)

In its rules and practices, the Senate always has emphasized the importance of maintaining decorum in its proceedings. "At no stage of the Senate's proceedings may a Senator "refer offensively to any State of the Union." "No Senator in debate shall, directly or indirectly, by any form of words impute to another Senator or to other Senators any conduct or motive unworthy or unbecoming a Senator." "No Senator shall interrupt another in debate without his consent, and to obtain such consent he shall first address the Presiding Officer; and no Senator shall speak more than twice upon any one question in debate on the same day without leave of the

Senate, which shall be determined without debate." "If any Senator, in speaking or otherwise, transgress the rules of the Senate, the Presiding officer shall, or any Senator may, call him to order; and when a Senator shall be called to order he shall sit down, and not proceed without leave of the Senate, which, if granted, shall be upon motion that he be allowed to proceed in order, which motion shall be determined without debate."

3

FORMS OF LEGISLATIVE BUSINESS

All proposed legislation, and nearly all formal actions by either of the two Houses, take the form of a bill or resolution.

A bill is a legislative proposal of a general nature. A bill may propose either a public or private matter, but both are numbered in the same sequence. Public bills are the most numerous. Private bills are designed to affect or benefit specific individuals or groups of individuals. Together, bills account for a large majority of the total of legislative proposals of each Congress. The Senate numbers bills in sequence starting with number 1, and each number is preceded by the designation "S". House bills are similarly numbered and prefaced by "H.R." Thus, bill number 100 in the Senate is written S. 100, and in the House, H.R. 100.

Joint resolutions, which have the same effect as bills unless they are used to propose amendments to the Constitution, are designated "S.J. Res. _____." Concurrent resolutions, which are designated "S. Con. Res. _____" for Senate concurrent resolutions, are chosen to express the sense of the Congress to the President or other parties; to attend to "housekeeping" matters affecting both Houses, such as the creation of a joint committee; or to carry proposals to correct the language of measures passed by one House (an engrossment) or both Houses (an enrollment). All concurrent resolutions, including corrective resolutions, must be agreed to in both the Senate and House. One House may seek to correct a measure it passed, or both Houses may wish to correct a measure awaiting the President's signature.

The former may be accomplished merely by specifying what changes or additions are to be made and requesting the other House to make them, or requesting the return of the measure to the originating House for that purpose. Correction of measures already sent to the President, however, are made after agreement of both Houses to concurrent resolutions requesting return of the measures from the White House. Such resolutions include a resolve that if and when a measure is returned, the action of the Presiding Officers of the two Houses in signing the measure shall be deemed rescinded, and the Secretary of the Senate or the Clerk of the House is authorized and directed in the re-enrollment of the measure to make the necessary corrections. The corrected measure (bill or joint resolution) is then again signed by the Secretary of the Senate or the Clerk of the House, the Speaker, and the Vice President and again delivered to the White House.

Finally there is the designation of "S. Res. _____" for Senate resolutions, which are used primarily to express the sense of the Senate only, or to take care of "housekeeping" matters, including changes in rules, that apply only to the Senate.

When the question of agreement to, or formal acceptance of, a resolution is raised, concurrent and simple resolutions are agreed to or adopted, whereas bills and joint resolutions are passed.

In the House of Representatives, measures have the following designations: "H.R. _____," for House bills; "H.J.Res. _____," for House joint resolutions; "H. Con. Res. _____," for House concurrent resolutions; and "H. Res. _____," for House resolutions. Bills and resolutions are numbered ad seriatim, in the chronological order in which they are introduced or submitted.

Senate and House bills and joint resolutions, when passed by both Houses in identical form and approved by the President, become public or private law—public laws affect the Nation as a whole; private laws benefit only an individual or a class thereof. The procedure on each is identical, with the exception of joint resolutions proposing amendments to the Constitution of the United States, which under the Constitution must be passed in each House by a two-thirds vote of the Members present and voting, a quorum being present. They are not sent to the President for his approval but to the Administrator of the General Services Administration, who transmits them to the various States. Constitutional amendments are valid when ratified by at least three-fourths of the States.

Concurrent resolutions have the force of both Houses and must be approved by them in identical form to be effective. However, they are not presented to the White House for the President's signature, because they do not become law. They are not signed by the President nor by the Speaker and the Vice President. Instead, they are attested by the Secretary of the Senate and Clerk of the House and transmitted after approval to the Administrator of the General Services Administration for publication in the Statutes at Large.

A House or Senate resolution (H. Res. _____ or S. Res. _____) only has the force of the House passing it, and action by the one House is all that is necessary.

4

ORIGINS OF LEGISLATION

Legislation originates in several ways. The Constitution provides that the President "shall from time to time give to the Congress Information of the State of the Union, and recommend to their Consideration such Measures as he shall judge necessary and expedient;..."

The President fulfills this duty either by personally addressing a joint session of the two Houses or by sending messages in writing to Congress, or to either body thereof, which are received and referred to the appropriate committees. The President usually presents or submits his annual message on the state of the Union shortly after the beginning of a session.

In addition, there are many executive communications sent to Congress. These are documents signed by the President or by an agency or department head, and filed or submitted as a report to the Senate as directed by law or otherwise. These items are numbered sequentially for a Congress and assigned a prefix EC. They are described only by a brief statement of the contents in the Congressional Record.

The right of petition is guaranteed the citizens of the United States by the Constitution, and many individual petitions as well as memorials from State legislatures are sent to Congress. They are laid before the two Houses by their respective Presiding Officers or submitted by individual Members of the House and Senate in their respective bodies, and are usually referred to the appropriate committees of the House in which they were submitted.

Bills to carry out the recommendations of the President are usually introduced "by request" by the chairmen of the various committees or subcommittees thereof which have jurisdiction of the subject matter. Sometimes the committees themselves may submit and report to the Senate "original bills" to carry out such recommendations.

The ideas for legislative proposals may come from an individual Representative or Senator, from any of the executive departments of the Government, from private organized groups or associations, or from any individual citizen. However, they can be introduced in their respective Houses only by Senators and Representatives. When introduced, they are referred to the standing committees which have jurisdiction over the subject matter.

Members frequently introduce bills that are similar in purpose, in which case the committee considering them may add to one of the bills the best features of the others for reporting to the parent body, or draft an entirely new bill (known as an original bill) and report it in lieu of the others.

5

BEGINNING A DAILY SESSION OF THE SENATE

Each day in the Senate begins as the Secretary of the Senate and the Presiding Officer for that day escort the Chaplain of the Senate or guest chaplain to the desk. The Chaplain is a clergyman chosen by the Senate, whose responsibility is to offer the prayer at the opening of each daily session, as well as to officiate at various ceremonies and respond to Senators' private needs.

CALENDAR AND LEGISLATIVE DAYS

As the Senate begins its new day, it is important to note that the Senate recognizes two meanings for the word "day," the "calendar" day and the "legislative" day. A calendar day is recognized as each 24 hour period. Reference may be made to a day certain, as in a unanimous consent request to vote on passage of a measure on August 4, 1996 (a specific, determined, or fixed day), or a day not yet determined, as in a unanimous consent request or rule requiring action "on either of the next two days of actual session." The references in these cases are to calendar days. A legislative day is the period of time following an adjournment of the Senate until another adjournment. A recess (rather than an adjournment) in no way affects a legislative day; therefore, one legislative day may consume a considerable period of time—days, weeks, even months—but one or more adjournments from one day to the next would cause the calendar and legislative day to coincide.

As used in the Rules of the Senate, a day generally is recognized as a legislative day unless specified as a calendar day. There is, for example, the proviso that "no Senator shall speak more than twice upon any one question in debate on the same legislative day..." in Rule XIX. However, Rule V, disallowing motions "to suspend, modify or amend any rule..., except on one day's notice in writing...," although not specifying the type of day, is interpreted as meaning one calendar day.

Morning Hour and Morning Business

The Senate Majority Leader by unanimous consent customarily provides for a brief period of time (usually 10 minutes each) at the beginning of each daily session for himself and the Minority Leader to be used at their discretion for observations on current events or pending legislation, submission and agreement of various legislative matters, etc. They may yield all or part of their time to their Senators for sundry purposes. It is with these orders that the day of the Senate begins.

During the morning hour of each legislative day, Rule VII of the Senate provides that, after the Journal is read, the Presiding Officer lay before the Senate messages, reports, and communications of various types.

Measures or matters are transmitted between the two Houses, as are written messages from one House to the other pertaining to the passage of measures or other conduct of official business requiring concurrence or notification. The President of the United States transmits written messages to the Congress, which are brought to the Chamber and announced to the Senate by a messenger from the White House. Such messages are numbered sequentially for a Congress and assigned a prefix PM. They are printed in full in the Congressional Record. Messages from the President may be received at any stage of Senate proceedings, except during votes or quorum calls, while the Journal is being read, or while a question of order or a motion to adjourn is pending.

The Presiding Officer then calls for the "presentation of petitions and memorials." These are documents memorializing the Government to do or not to do something. Memorials and petitions when laid before the Senate are numbered and assigned a prefix POM, and all memorials and petitions from State, Territorial, and insular possession legislatures or conventions, lawfully called, are printed in full in the Record when presented. Those received from other memorialists or petitioners are described only by a brief statement of the contents.

Next the Presiding Officer calls for the filing of reports of committees, the introduction of bills and joint resolutions, and the submission of other resolutions. Under recent practices, however, nearly all bills, resolutions, and committee reports are presented by Senators to the clerks at the Presiding Officer's desk for processing throughout the day, and without any comments from the floor.

PRESENTING MEASURES

The Majority Leader customarily secures unanimous consent at the beginning of each new Congress to allow receipt at the desk of all measures on days when morning business is conducted. Such permission allows Senators to bring measures to the desk at any time during the day, instead of following the procedure as set forth in Rule VII, requiring introduction of bills and joint resolutions only on a new legislative day during the transaction of morning business, followed by submission of other resolutions.

Bills and resolutions still may be introduced from the floor, however, and any Senator, when doing so, usually discusses his proposal when he presents it. There can be only one prime sponsor of a bill or resolution, but commonly other Senators are included as cosponsors.

The Senate's rules make no mention of multiple sponsorship, which has been a common practice for many years. Though custom permits unlimited numbers of Senators to sponsor a wide assortment of measures, it prohibits more than one Member's name to appear on a reported bill or resolution and the printed report accompanying it. Co-sponsors are often shown on measures as introduced, but other names may be added, by unanimous consent, at their next printing. Since its inception, the advisability of multiple sponsorship has been questioned by many Senators, and others have submitted resolutions to abolish the practice. The Committee on Rules and Administration has held hearings and favorably reported measures to amend the Rules to prohibit joint sponsorship, except under limited conditions, but to date, the full Senate has not voted its approval or disapproval. A former practice of holding measures at the desk for days, to permit the addition of names, has often met considerable opposition and was discontinued in the 1960s.

Measures can be submitted with the phrase "by request," a term found following the names of the sponsors of bills and resolutions that are introduced or submitted at the request of the Administration or private organizations or individuals. Such proposals, though introduced as a courtesy, are not necessarily favored by the Senators sponsoring them. Drafts of proposed legislation from the President or an executive agency are usually introduced by the chairman of the committee of jurisdiction, who may be of the opposition party.

6

MOTIONS QUORUMS, AND VOTES

MOTIONS

The motions which "shall be received" under Rule XXII when "a question is pending" "and which shall have precedence as they stand arranged" are:

- To adjourn.
- To adjourn to a day certain, or that when the Senate adjourn it shall be to a day certain.
- To take a recess.
- To proceed to the consideration of executive business.
- To lay on the table.
- To postpone indefinitely.
- To postpone to a day certain.
- To commit.
- To amend.

All but the last four of these motions are not debatable.

The motion to adjourn should be distinguished from a resolution to adjourn both houses of Congress. Neither is debatable. The Senate may adjourn for as long a period of time as it sees fit, up to the Constitutional limitation of three days, without the consent of the other House, or it may adjourn for only a few minutes and reconvene on a new legislative day in the same calendar day.

The motion to lay on the table is a simple way of taking final action on pending business on which the Senate wishes to take a negative position. It is applicable to a bill and amendments thereto as well as to certain motions. An amendment can be laid on the table without prejudice to the bill to which it was offered, but an amendment to the amendment would also go to the table. Since the motion is not debatable, the question can be brought to a vote in a hurry. The motion is used generally to reach a final disposition on motions to reconsider or appeals from the decision of the chair. While the motion is applicable to pending business, it is not commonly used for the disposition of legislation—bills are generally either voted up or down. The preamble to a bill or resolution may be laid on the table without carrying the bill or resolution with it.

The motion to postpone indefinitely is the next in order, but it is rarely used to dispose of bills except in the case of companion bills, i.e., the Senate passes a House-passed bill and indefinitely postpones a companion Senate bill which has been reported and placed on the calendar. It is a way of effecting a final disposition of a measure. The motion to postpone to a day certain is also used by the Senate. These motions are debatable and amendable and take precedence over a motion to refer or commit. A motion to take up another bill while unfinished business is pending has precedence over a motion to postpone the unfinished business to a day certain.

A motion to recommit a bill to committee with instructions to report the bill back forthwith with an amendment, if agreed to, requires that the committee report the bill back to the Senate immediately with that proposed amendment which is then before the Senate for consideration.

The last of this series of motions which shall be received under Rule XXII, "when a question is pending," and in the order listed above, is "to amend." Any bill, or amendment thereto, before the Senate is open to amendment.

Quorums

"If, at any time during the daily sessions of the Senate, a question shall be raised by any Senator as to the presence of a quorum, the Presiding Officer shall forthwith direct the Secretary to call the roll and shall announce the result, and these proceedings shall be without debate." "Whenever upon such roll call it shall be ascertained that a quorum is not present, a majority of the Senators present may direct the Sergeant at Arms to request, and, when necessary, to compel the attendance of the absent Senators, which order shall be determined without debate; and pending its execution, and until a quorum shall be present, no debate nor motion, except to adjourn, shall be in order."

The Senate proceeds under the assumption that a quorum is present unless the question is raised; in that case, the bells are rung to inform the "absentee" Senators and the Presiding Officer directs a call of the roll. All decisions incident thereto are made without debate, and if a quorum is not present by the time the results from the roll call are announced, a majority of the Senators present may direct the Sergeant at Arms to request or compel the attendance of the absent Senators. Senators may be forced to attend, unless granted a "leave of absence" or by authority of the Senate, even if a quorum is present. Senators who do not reach the chamber when the roll is being called in time to answer to their names may gain recognition after the call and have their presence or vote recorded, provided the results have not been announced.

Under the practice of the Senate, anyone, once recognized, can request a quorum call, but a Senator who has the floor cannot be forced to yield to another for that purpose. The chair is not permitted to count in order to ascertain the presence of a quorum; it must be determined by roll call.

There is no limit to the number of requests for quorum calls that may be made during the course of a day; a request is generally held dilatory if no business has transpired since the last one, and it is not in order immediately after a roll call vote showing that a quorum is present. The reception of a message from the House has not been ruled as the transaction of business sufficient to justify a quorum call. The following have been ruled to be business: the ordering of engrossment and third reading of a joint resolution, presentation and reference of a communication, granting of permission to insert an article in the Record, objection to a bill under call of the calendar under Rule VIII, the making of a motion or ordering of the yeas and nays, voting on motions to recess, adjourn, and lay on table and on an appeal from the decision of the chair, the offering of an amendment, agreeing to a motion for an executive session, and submitting a report out of order.

A motion may be made to request attendance of those absent, and instructions to compel their attendance may be added. Such a motion is not debatable. A quorum call on various occasions has been withdrawn by unanimous consent while the roll was being called; but when an announcement of no quorum has been made, it is not in order to vacate the call even by unanimous consent. In the absence of a quorum, neither debate nor the transaction of business, including motions (except the motion to adjourn), is in order; it is not even in order to move to recess.

VOTING

Rule XII, relating to voting, provides:

1. When the yeas and nays are ordered, the names of Senators shall be called alphabetically; and each Senator shall, without debate, declare his assent or dissent to the question, unless excused by the Senate, and no Senator shall be permitted to vote after the decision shall have been announced by the Presiding Officer, but may for sufficient reasons, with unanimous consent, change or withdraw his vote. No motion to suspend this rule shall be in order, nor shall the Presiding Officer entertain any request to suspend it by unanimous consent.

2. When a Senator declines to vote on call of his name, he shall be required to assign his reasons therefore, and having assigned them, the Presiding Officer shall submit the question to the Senate: "Shall the Senator, for the reasons assigned by him, be excused from voting?" which shall be decided without debate; and these proceedings shall be had after the roll call and before the result is announced; and any further proceedings in reference thereto shall be after such announcement.

Any one of the several methods of voting utilized by the Senate may be resorted to for final disposition of any amendment or bill or question. The methods are: voice vote, division, and yea and nay. The yeas and nays may be ordered when the request is seconded by 1/5 of a presumptive quorum, but frequently the Presiding Officer does not bother to count; he merely takes a glance at the "showing" of hands and orders the call; simultaneously the bells ring in both the Senate wing of the Capitol and the Senate office buildings. The names of the

Senators are called in their alphabetical order. Voting and changes of votes are in order until the decision has been announced by the chair.

A Senator can change his vote at any time before the result is announced. In the case of a veto, a yea and nay vote is required by the Constitution. Otherwise, the Senators may utilize any of the methods. After the result of a vote has been announced, a request for a division or yea and nay vote comes too late; the announcement that the "ayes (or nays) seem to have it" is not a final result. The yeas and nays may be demanded prior to announcement of the results of a division vote.

Where less than a quorum votes and the number of pairs announced are not sufficient to make a quorum, it is the duty of the chair to order a quorum call; the vote is valid if a quorum was present, even if a quorum did not vote, provided that a number of those not voting, sufficient to make a quorum, announced they were present but paired.

"Pairing" is the practice that has been developed in both houses to enable Representatives and Senators to register their opinion on any particular issue or issues when they are unavoidably absent from the chamber on public or private business. By the use of "pairs" a Senator (or Representative) favoring a particular issue, and who is absent when a roll-call vote is taken on it, may make his opinion effective by contracting (pairing) with a colleague opposing the issue that neither of the Senators will vote. "Pairs" are not counted as yeas or nays in the official tabulation of the roll call for the purpose of determining the adoption or rejection of the issue being voted on.

After all amendments to an original amendment to a bill have been disposed of, the question recurs on the adoption of the amendment as amended, if amended. After all amendments to a bill have been acted on, the question recurs on third reading and passage of the bill. After the Senate acts on an amendment or on a bill, or almost any question on which the Senate has voted, any Senator voting on the side that prevailed may offer a motion to reconsider the vote by which that action was taken. A Senator voting in the minority cannot move to reconsider a yea and nay vote; if he did not vote he may.

7

SENATE OFFICIALS ON THE FLOOR

Various officials are present on the floor of the Senate when it convenes, including the Majority and Minority Leaders of the Senate, the Secretary and Assistant Secretary of the Senate, the Sergeant at Arms, the Legislative Clerk, the Journal Clerk, the Parliamentarian of the Senate, the Secretaries for the Majority and the Minority, the Official Reporters of Debate, and the Pages.

The Secretary of the Senate is the elected official of the Senate responsible for management of many legislative and administrative services. The Secretary is the disbursing officer for the Senate. The official seal of the Senate is in the custody of, and its use is prescribed by, the Secretary. In the absence of the Vice President, and pending the election of a President pro tempore, the Secretary performs the duties of the chair.

The Assistant Secretary is the chief assistant to the Secretary of the Senate. The Assistant Secretary performs the functions of the Secretary in the latter's absence, and in the event of the death or resignation of the Secretary would act as Secretary in all matters except those duties as disbursing officer of the Senate.

On the day after the first organization of the Senate, a Doorkeeper was chosen whose title was eventually changed to Sergeant at Arms. His duties are to execute the Senate's orders as to decorum on the floor and in the galleries. He is responsible for the enforcement of all rules made for the regulation of the Senate wing of the Capitol. He also is the custodian of all properties under the dominion of the Senate and supervises the messengers, pages and other workers who serve the Senate. If the Senate decides to issue warrants of arrest for its absent Members, it is the duty of the Sergeant of Arms to bring those Senators into custody.

Article 1, section 5, paragraph 3 of the Constitution provides that "Each House shall keep a Journal of its Proceedings, and from time to time publish the same, excepting such Parts as may in their Judgment require Secrecy; and the Yeas and Nays of the Members of either House and any question shall, at the Desire of one-fifth of those Present be entered on the Journal." The Journal Clerk is charged with maintaining the Senate Journal under the direction of the Secretary of the Senate.

The Legislative Clerk is responsible for reporting all bills, messages from the House, conference reports, and amendments to the Senate. All record votes are taken by the Legislative Clerk and his assistants.

An appointed official of the Senate, the Parliamentarian functions under the direction of the Secretary of the Senate. The Parliamentarian's chief duty and responsibility is to advise the Presiding Officer on parliamentary aspects of Senate activity. The Parliamentarian advises Senators and senatorial committee staffs, and is called upon by other branches of Government, the press, and the public for information regarding procedural aspects of Senate activity.

The Official Reporters of Debates prepare the material concerning business of the Senate for inclusion in the Congressional Record. All proceedings in the Senate Chamber are reported verbatim by a staff of Official Reporters, who are under the supervision of the Editor in Chief. The Editor in Chief is the editor of all matter contained in the Senate proceedings. In addition to the verbatim proceedings in the Senate Chamber, the office of the Official Reporters processes for inclusion in the Congressional Record a description of the morning business conducted by the Senate (measures introduced, messages from the President and the House of Representatives, co-sponsors, communications received, and notices of hearings), and additional or unspoken statements of Senators. The Official Reporters of Debates are appointed by the Secretary of the Senate.

The Secretary for the Majority is an elected officer of the Senate who is responsible for providing many support services to the majority party leaders and members of the Senate. The floor-related duties of the Secretary include supervising the cloakroom, briefing Senators on votes and issues that are under consideration on the floor, obtaining pairs for Senators, and polling Senators when the Leadership so desires. Additionally, the Secretary is responsible for assigning Senate Chamber seats to the majority party Members; maintaining a file of committee assignment requests; staffing the committee which arranges majority party committee assignments; recommending to the Leadership majority party candidates for appointment to boards, commissions, and international conferences; maintaining records of such appointments; providing a repository for official minutes of majority party conferences and meetings of the Policy Committee, Steering Committee, and committee chairmen; monitoring the nominations on the Executive Calendar; and other duties as directed by the Leadership.

The Secretary for the Minority also is an elected officer of the Senate, and performs corresponding duties for the minority party leaders and other Senators.

The Republican Legislative Scheduling Office provides floor assistance to Republican Senators. The staff serves as a liaison between Republican Senators and the Republican leadership in dealing with Senators' legislative interests, unanimous consent requests, time agreements, and the scheduling of the Senate's proceedings. When the Republicans are in the majority, the Republican Legislative Scheduling Office also schedules Republican Senators to preside over the Senate.

Floor assistance for Democratic Senators is provided by the staff of the Democratic Policy Committee. This staff is available to provide information regarding the scheduling of legislation and to act as liaison between the legislative committees and the Democratic leadership. Assistance is given in the arrangement of unanimous consent requests on time agreements, amendments, and procedural issues on legislation being debated by the Senate. In addition, the staff provides advice on general parliamentary situations.

The Democratic Policy Committee provides other services to Democratic Senators, including detailed voting records for each Democratic Senator, an annual report on the major achievements of the session; an extensive index of record votes on legislation, both chronologically and by subject matter, and briefings on major bills and amendments.

Its counterpart, the Senate Republican Policy Committee, provides similar services for Republican Senators: maintenance of a research library; publication of legislative notices summarizing bills and resolutions on the Senate Calendar and proposed amendments thereto; publication of detailed analysis of all Senate record votes plus indexes, annual abstracts, and lists of voice votes; publication of the weekly Republican Counsel's Report; publication of policy papers on major issues; development of Republican legislative initiatives; research, legislative analysis, and speech writing for Republican Senators upon request; personnel placement and counseling; briefing officials from State and local governments on national issues; assisting new Senators with staff orientation; producing the information on the special television channel containing in-house updates on the Senate schedule; and assistance to the party leader in preparation of the End-of-Year Report.

Senate pages, male and female, when appointed, must be juniors in high school. They may not be appointed or serve after attaining the age of 17, except that if they are serving and enrolled in the Page School, they may continue their service through the session of the Senate in which the Page School terminates.

Riding Page Service is provided by a separate service, through the Senate Post Office, several times a day for delivery of Senators' letters to major Federal agencies in the District of Columbia only.

8

SENATE COMMITTEE CONSIDERATION

Senate committees are appointed by resolution at the beginning of each Congress, with power to continue and act until their successors are appointed. All Senate committees are created by the Senate. At present, Senate committees include 16 standing committees, three select committees, and one special committee. Standing committees are charged to report by bill or otherwise on matters within a defined jurisdiction and generally to study and review, on a comprehensive basis, certain matters relating thereto. Select and special committees have varying powers and obligations, and increasingly have been given legislative jurisdiction. In current practice, the committee chairman is a member of the majority party. He or she is chosen by order of the Senate, and is usually, but not always, the senior Member in point of service of the majority Members of the committee.

Senate Members may also serve, along with House Members, on joint committees, whose duties and responsibilities are set forth in the respective resolutions or laws creating them. There are currently four joint committees of the Congress. Conference committees, appointed when there is disagreement to a measure after passage by both Houses, are composed of Members of both the Senate and House, like joint committees, but votes in a conference committee are not as a body, but as two delegations.

9

COMMITTEE RULES

Rule XXVI on committee procedure provides that each committee shall adopt rules (not inconsistent with the Standing Rules of the Senate) governing the procedure of such committee. It provides also that the rules of each committee shall be published in the Congressional Record not later than March 1 of each year, except that if any such committee is established on or after February 1 of a year, the rules of that committee during the year of establishment shall be published in the Record within 60 days. An amendment to a committee's rules shall be published in the Record not later than 30 days after the adoption of the amendment.

Committees as a rule have regular meeting days, but they may meet at the call of their chairmen or upon the request of a majority at other times. At these meetings matters on the committee calendar are usually the order of business, but any matter within the committee's jurisdiction may be considered—for example, an investigation of an agency of the Government over which the committee has jurisdiction, or a hearing at which an official discusses policies and operations of his agency.

Once a bill has been introduced and has been referred by the Presiding Officer with the advice of the Parliamentarian, the clerk of the committee enters it upon the committee's Calendar of Business. Any committee may refer its pending bills to its subcommittees for study and reports thereon. Most of the committees have standing subcommittees, and frequently ad hoc subcommittees are appointed to study and report on particular pieces of legislation or to make a study of a certain subject.

Committees or subcommittees generally hold hearings on all major or controversial legislation before drafting the proposal into a final form for reporting to the Senate. The length of hearings and the number of witnesses testifying vary, depending upon the time available, the number of witnesses wanting to be heard, the desires of the committee to hear witnesses, etc. Recommendations of the Administration, in conjunction with the Office of Management and Budget, are sought by the committees on nearly all major legislation, but they are in no way obligated to accept such recommendations.

For example, the Department of Agriculture's Office of Governmental and Public Affairs, providing liaison between the department and the Congress, would be addressed on a bill relating to inspection of livestock, meat, and agricultural products, and the Office of Congressional Affairs of the General Services Administration would be asked to comment on proposed legislation affecting small business, disadvantaged business, and related subcontracting programs. The responses are often used in support of or against matters pending before the Senate by being quoted on the floor or being inserted in the Record by Senators during debate.

A subcommittee makes reports to its full committee, and the latter may adopt such reports without change, amend them in any way it desires, reject them, or adopt an entirely different report.

At a committee's "mark up" session, usually held just prior to reporting a bill or resolution back to the full Senate, the committee makes its final decisions about the content and form of the measure. The full committee then may report it to the Senate favorably with or without amendments, submit an adverse report thereon, or vote not to report on anything.

The measure can be reported with committee amendments which may (a) insert, (b) strike, (c) strike part of the bill and insert other language, or (d) strike the entire text and insert a complete substitute, thereby rejecting *in toto* the language of the measure as it was referred to, considered by, and reported by the Senate committee. The desired changes in the measure are indicated in the reprinted measure by use of italic type for additions and line-type for strike-outs, in contrast to the original introduced form of the measure which is printed in roman type.

Included may be additions, corrections, or modifications to the preamble of a resolution—the part(s) of a measure prefaced by the word "Whereas," which precedes the resolving clause. These are voted on after passage or adoption of the measure. Such clauses, which are introductory statements declaring the reasons for and the intent of the legislation, if amended, would reflect changes or modifications contained in the text of the measure. Also, the title may be amended.

Committees need not act on all bills referred to them. Under the Senate's rules, a Senator may enter a motion to discharge a committee from the further consideration of any bill, but this is rarely done. By unanimous consent, some bills are discharged from one committee and sent to another. If a motion to discharge is agreed to, the bill is thereby taken out of the jurisdiction of that committee and placed on the Senate Calendar of Business. It may subsequently be referred to another committee.

10

COMMITTEE REPORTS

The chairman, or some other member of the committee designated for that purpose, reports bills to the Senate, and when reported they are placed on the Senate Calendar of Business, unless unanimous consent is given for immediate consideration.

The action taken by the committee appears on the copy of the bill reported, and a written report, which is numbered ad seriatim, nearly always accompanies the bill. The reports, like the bills, are printed by the Government Printing Office for distribution.

A reported bill passes through the same channels in the Secretary's Office as an introduced bill, for notation of the proper entries in the Senate's official records. The bill also is reprinted, showing the calendar and report numbers, the name of the Senator reporting it, the date, and whether the committee ordered it reported with or without amendment. Committee members may write their own minority, supplemental, and/or additional views on the bill, and these statements are printed as a part of the committee report on the measure.

11

CONSIDERING MEASURES ON THE SENATE FLOOR

The Senate's Majority and Minority Leaders, as the spokesmen for their parties, and in consultation with their respective policy committees, implement and direct the legislative schedule and program.

Most measures are passed either on the call of the Calendar or by unanimous consent procedure. The more significant and controversial matters are considered, when possible, under unanimous consent agreements limiting debate and controlling time on the measure, amendments thereto, and debatable motions relating to it. This is done because otherwise debate is unlimited. Measures may be brought up on motion by a simple majority vote if they have been on the Calendar one legislative day. Such a motion to proceed is usually made by the Majority Leader or his designee and is usually debatable. The motion to proceed to the consideration of a measure on the Calendar is usually only made if there has been objection to a unanimous consent request to proceed to its consideration.

On highly controversial matters, the Senate frequently has to resort to cloture to work its will. Under Rule XXII, if three-fifths of the Senators duly chosen and sworn (60 if the Senate is at full membership of 100) vote in the affirmative, further debate on the question shall be limited to no more than one hour for each Senator, and the time for consideration of the matter shall be limited to 30 additional hours, unless increased by another three-fifths vote. On a measure or motion to amend the Senate Rules, it takes two-thirds of the Senators present and voting, a quorum being present, to invoke cloture.

Under Rule VIII, which governs the consideration of bills on the call of the Senate Calendar, there is supposed to be a Calendar call each day at the end of the morning business. Under current practice, however, this very rarely occurs; instead, the Calendar is usually called, if at all, pursuant to a unanimous consent order. Rule VII makes a call of the Calendar mandatory on Monday if the Senate had adjourned after its prior sitting. This requirement may only be waived by unanimous consent, and it has become the regular practice of the leadership to request that the requirement be waived.

12

THE AMENDMENT PROCESS

Once a bill or resolution is before the Senate, it is subject to the amendatory process, both by the committee reporting it and by individual Senators offering amendments from the floor. A committee amendment reported as a total substitute (striking all after the enacting clause and inserting new language for the entire bill) for the pending measure is always voted on last, inasmuch as once a total substitute is agreed to, further amendments are precluded. With this exception, however, committee amendments take priority and are considered in order as they appear in the printed copy of the measure before the Senate. The only amendments from the floor in order during the consideration of these committee amendments are amendments to the committee amendments or sometimes to the part of the bill the committee amendments would affect.

Once the committee amendments have been disposed of, however, any Senator may propose amendments to any part of the bill not already amended, and while an amendment is pending, an amendment to the amendment is in order. By precedent, an amendment to an amendment to an amendment, being an amendment in the third degree, is not in order. However, the first amendment in the nature of a substitute for a bill, whether reported by a committee or offered by an individual Senator, is considered an original question and is amendable in two more degrees.

There are certain special procedures in the Senate which limit the amendatory process. For example, during the consideration of general appropriation bills, amendments are subject to the strictures of Rule XVI under which it is not in order to offer non-germane amendments or amendments proposing new or general legislation or increasing the amount of an appropriation if that increase has not been previously authorized or estimated for in the President's budget. Likewise, when operating under a general unanimous consent agreement in the usual form on a bill or resolution, amendments must be germane. Germaneness of amendments is also required once the Senate has invoked cloture; in addition, any amendments considered under cloture must have been submitted in writing before the Senate's vote on cloture.

13

FINAL PASSAGE

When all committee amendments and all Senators' floor amendments have been disposed of, the bill is ordered engrossed and read a third time, which step ends the amendatory process. The third reading is by title only. The question is then put upon passage of the bill, which requires a simple majority vote. If a resolution has a preamble, it may be agreed to, amended, or stricken out after the resolution has been adopted. The title to a bill is also acted upon after its passage; the title may be amended if amendments made to the bill necessitate such a change. At any time before its passage, a bill may be laid on the table or postponed indefinitely, either of which motions has the effect of killing the bill. Alternatively, a bill may be made a special order for a day certain, which requires a two-thirds vote; laid aside temporarily; recommitted to the committee which reported the bill; referred to a different committee; or displaced by taking up another bill by a majority vote.

Most bills are passed by a voice vote only, but where a doubt is raised in such a case, the Presiding Officer, or any Senator, before the result is announced, may request a division of the Senate to determine the question. Before the result of a voice or division vote has been announced, a roll-call vote may be had upon the demand of one-fifth of the Senators present, but at least 11—one fifth of the presumptive quorum of 51.

In the case of a yea-and-nay vote, any Senator who voted with the prevailing side or who did not vote may, on the same calendar day or on either of the next two days the Senate is actually in session, make a motion to reconsider the question. On a voice vote or division vote, however, any Senator may make the motion. If made before other business intervenes, it may be proceeded with and is debatable. It may be laid on the table without prejudice to the main question and is a final disposition of the motion. A majority vote determines questions of reconsideration. If the motion is agreed to, another vote may be taken on the question reconsidered; if disagreed to, the first decision of the Senate is affirmed. The making of such a motion is privileged but may not be made while another matter is pending before the Senate.

Only one motion to reconsider the same question is in order. Such a motion, under rule XIII, may be withdrawn by the mover by leave of the Senate, which may be granted by a majority vote or by unanimous consent.

A bill cannot be transmitted to the House of Representatives while a motion to reconsider remains unacted upon.

14

ENGROSSMENT AND TRANSMITTAL TO THE HOUSE

The printed bill used at the desk by the Senate during its consideration is the official desk copy, showing the amendments adopted, if any. Once it is endorsed as having passed, it is sent to the Secretary's Office and delivered to the Bill Clerk. After making the proper entries on his records and the data retrieval system, the Bill Clerk turns it over to the Enrolling Clerk who makes an appropriate entry on his records and sends it to the Government Printing Office to be printed on special white paper in the form in which it passed the Senate. This printed Act is attested by the Secretary as having passed the Senate as of the proper date, and is termed the official engrossed bill.

After the passage of a bill by one body, it technically becomes an Act (not yet effective as a law), but it nevertheless continues to generally referred to as a bill.

Engrossed bills are transmitted, or "messaged", to the House of Representatives by one of the clerks in the Secretary's Office, who is announced by one of the House's officials. Upon being recognized by the Speaker, the clerk announces that the Senate has passed a bill (giving its number and title) in which the concurrence of the House is requested.

Upon receipt of such a message from the Senate, the Speaker refers the measures contained therein to appropriate committees. If, however, a substantially similar House bill already has been favorably reported by a committee, the Senate bill, unless it creates a charge upon the Treasury, may remain on the Speaker's table instead of being referred to committee. It may subsequently be taken up or its text may be substituted for that of the House bill when consideration of the latter occurs.

15

House Committee Consideration

Senate bills and resolutions when messaged to the House may be referred by the Speaker to the appropriate House committee, just as he refers all bills and resolutions introduced in the House. If referred, they are processed in much the same fashion as in the Senate—that is, endorsed for reference, recorded in the Journal, listed in the Congressional Record, and printed by the Government Printing Office for distribution. House committees, like Senate committees, have committee calendars of business and regular meeting days (but may also meet on the call of their chairman) for the consideration of business pending before them.

The procedure of House committees in considering and reporting bills also is much the same as that of the Senate committees; for example, they too have standing subcommittees and ad hoc subcommittees. In contrast to the Senate, however, House rules allow the Speaker, under some circumstances, to refer a bill to two or more committees in sequence, or to refer parts of the same bill to different committees, when more than one committee has jurisdiction over the subject matter contained in the bill.

After all House committees having jurisdiction have concluded consideration of a bill, it may be reported to the House with or without amendments. A written report accompanies each reported measure. When reported from committee, a bill is placed on the Union or House Calendar, if a public bill, or on the Private Calendar. The House also has a Corrections Calendar, on which are placed bills that are expected to enjoy considerably more than majority support on the floor, and a calendar of motions to discharge committees from further consideration of bills referred to them.

16

HOUSE FLOOR ACTION

The House rules designate special legislative days which have been established to expedite certain types of unprivileged business. The special legislative days are: Calendar Wednesday (every Wednesday), District of Columbia (the second and fourth Mondays), suspension of the rules (every Monday and Tuesday), and the Corrections Calendar (the first and third Mondays). Private Calendar business, if any, is considered on the first and third Tuesdays of each month, and discharge motions on the second and fourth Mondays.

Generally speaking, after the regular routine business each morning, including the approval of the Journal, the House proceeds to the consideration of whatever bills or resolutions are to be acted on that day. The order varies somewhat, as follows: (1) On days set aside for certain procedures, such as suspension motions on Mondays and Tuesdays, bills and resolutions are called up in pursuance of the procedure, as defined by House rules in each instance; (2) under unanimous consent, bills are called up in pursuance of such requests made and granted by the House, regardless of the regular rules of procedure; and (3) privileged matters, such as general appropriation bills and conference reports, may be called up by the Members in charge of them at almost any time after they have lain over for three days, providing the Representative in charge is recognized by the Speaker.

The House also can determine the order of its business and decide what bill to take up by adopting a special rule (simple House resolution) reported by the Rules Committee. The procedure for consideration of such measures is defined in each instance in the special rule. A special rule to call up a bill may be debated for an hour before it is voted on. Bills called up under special rules are usually major or controversial pieces of legislation.

Bills which are first considered in the Committee of the Whole House on the State of the Union are considered for amendment under the 5-minute rule, after which the Committee of the Whole reports them back to the House for action on any amendments that may have been adopted, and then for the vote on final passage.

In the House, as in the Senate, bills are read three times before they are passed. After a Senate bill is passed by the House, with or without amendment, it is returned to the Senate; if there are amendments, the amendments are engrossed before being messaged to

the Senate. All House engrossments are printed on blue
paper.

17

MESSAGES AND AMENDMENTS BETWEEN THE HOUSES

SENATE ACTION ON HOUSE AMENDMENTS

Senate bills returned with House amendments are held at the desk and almost always are subsequently laid before the Senate by the Presiding Officer upon request or motion of a Senator (usually the Majority Leader or the manager of the bill). The Presiding Officer may also do this upon his own initiative, but this is rarely done. After the House message has been laid down, the House's amendments may be considered individually or, by unanimous consent, en bloc. Any one off the following motions relating to the amendment or amendments may then be offered, taking precedence in the order named : (1) a motion to refer the amendments to a standing committee of the Senate, (2) a motion to amend the amendments; (3) a motion to agree to the amendments; and (4) a motion to disagree to the amendments and ask a conference with the House. Usually number (4) includes authority for the Presiding Officer to appoint conferees on the part of the Senate, although the power to name conferees is in the Senate, not in the Chair. The number of conferees named varies widely. The usual range is 7 to 11, but occasionally a larger number is appointed, especially in the case of general appropriation bills or omnibus bills such as reconciliation measures.

In the case of motion number (2), the amendments made by the Senate to the House amendments are transmitted to the House, with a request for its concurrence therein. If the House concurs or agrees in all the amendments (the words being used synonymously), the legislative steps in the passage of the bill are completed. The House, however, may amend the Senate amendments to the House amendments, this being the second, and therefore the last, degree in which amendments between the Houses may be made. The House amendments, if any, are transmitted to the Senate, usually with a request for concurrence therein. As in the case of the original House amendments, the Senate may agree to some, disagree to others, or ask for a conference with the House thereon.

A conference may be requested at any stage of the consideration of these amendments between the houses. If, instead, the Senate agrees to all the House amendments to the Senate bill or to the Senate's amendments to House amendments, such action brings the two Houses into complete agreement, and likewise completes the legislative steps.

If the Senate refers the House amendments to a standing committee, the committee, after consideration, may recommend action indicated in motions (2), (3), or (4), and may make such a motion accordingly on the Senate floor.

BILLS ORIGINATING IN THE HOUSE

If a bill or resolution originates in the House, it follows the same steps as set forth above, except in reverse, i.e., a House committee considers it first; it is passed by the House; it is messaged to the Senate and referred to a Senate committee; the committee reports it to the Senate and it is then acted on by that body. If amended, it is returned to the House for its concurrence in the Senate amendments.

18

CONFERENCE COMMITTEES AND REPORTS

When the Senate requests a conference or agrees to the House's request for a conference and names its conferees, it informs the House of its action by message. After the second House agrees to the conference, appoints conferees, and apprises the first House of its action by message, all the papers relating to the measure sent to conference (referred to as the "official papers") are transmitted to the conference. This includes the original engrossed bill, engrossed amendments, and the various messages of transmittal between the Houses.

Since the conferees of each House vote as a unit, the House, like the Senate, may appoint as many conferees as it chooses to meet with the Senate conferees to reconcile the differences between the two Houses—the sole purpose of a conference. Thus, having a larger number of conferees than the other House does not provide an advantage.

After deliberation, the conferees may make one or more recommendations; for example, (1) that the House recede from all or certain of its amendments; (2) that the Senate recede from its disagreement to all or certain of the House amendments and agree to the same; or (3) that the conference committee report an inability to agree in all or in part. Usually, however, there is compromise.

Conferees dealing with an amendment or a series of amendments are more limited in their options than conferees dealing with a bill passed by the second House with an amendment in the nature of a substitute. They can only deal with the matters in disagreement. They cannot insert new matter or leave out matter agreed to by both Houses, and if they exceed their authority, a point of order will lie against the conference report. Each House may instruct its conferees, but this is rarely done. Such instructions are not binding since conferences are presumed to be full and free—one House cannot restrict the other House's conferees.

Where one House passes a bill of the other House with an amendment in the nature of a substitute and the measure then goes to conference, the conferees have wider latitude since the entire matter is in conference. They may report a third version on the same subject matter; all of its provisions, however, must be germane modifications of either the House or Senate version, or it will be subject to a point of order.

19

Senate and House Action on Conference Reports

The recommendations of the conferees are incorporated in a written report and a joint statement of managers, made in duplicate, both of which must be signed by a majority of the conferees of each House. If there are amendments upon which they were unable to agree, a statement to this effect is included in the report. These are referred to as amendments in disagreement. The conferees cannot report parts of amendments in disagreement. For example, conferees must report in full agreement or disagreement when a bill had gone to conference after one House had amended it with a complete substitute for the other House's text.

One report, together with the papers if the House is to act on it first, is taken by the House conferees, or managers, as they are termed in that body, and subsequently presented by them to the House, with an accompanying explanatory statement as to its effect upon the matters involved. The report must lie over three days in the House before it may be considered, except during the last six days of a session. The Senate conferees take the other copy which is presented for printing under the requirements of the Legislative Reorganization Act, as amended in 1970. To save time and expense, this requirement is frequently waived in the Senate by unanimous consent.

Normally, the House agreeing to a conference on a bill acts first on conference report, but either House can act first if it has the official papers. Conference reports are privileged in both the Senate and the House. They cannot be amended, but must be voted upon in their entirety. If amendments in disagreement were reported by the conferees, they are acted on after the conference report is adopted and may be subject to amendment. After adoption by the first House, the conference report is transmitted with the official papers to the other House with a message announcing its action.

Assuming action by the House first, the Senate conferees could then present their report and ask for its immediate consideration. It does not have to lie over for three days in the Senate, as it does in the House, and the motion to proceed to its consideration is not debatable; thus the Senate may act immediately. A motion to recommit a conference report may not be made in the second House acting on the report since the conferees of the first House were discharged when their body agreed to the report.

If conferees reach a complete agreement on all of the House amendments to a Senate bill, and the House adopts that report, the adoption of the report by the Senate completes the legislative action on the bill. If, however, there were amendments upon which an agreement had not been reached by the conferees, the adoption of the report by both Houses leaves the parliamentary status of these particular amendments in disagreement the same as if no conference had been held.

If the amendments on which an agreement could not be reached were House amendments, and the House acted first on the report, it could then recede from its amendments, eliminating the amendments in disagreement; then, if the Senate were to adopt the report, the bill would be cleared for the President's signature. If they were Senate amendments and the House acted first, the House could concur in the Senate amendments or concur in them with amendments. If the Senate amendments were concurred in by the House, that would clear the amendments in disagreement, and when the Senate agreed to the conference report, the bill would be cleared for the President's signature. If the House should concur in the Senate amendments reported in disagreement with its own House amendments, after the Senate agreed to the report, it could concur in the House amendments to the Senate amendments which would clear the bill for the President's signature.

If the amendments reported in disagreement are not so disposed of, a further conference on these amendments could be requested by one House and agreed to by the other. When this happens, the two Houses usually appoint the same conferees. Until all the amendments in disagreement are reconciled by the two Houses, the bill cannot be presented to the President.

If a conference report is rejected by one of the Houses, it so notifies the other body by message and usually requests another conference; however, it may merely notify the second body of its action without requesting a further conference, leaving further steps to be taken by the other House. Endorsements showing these various legislative steps, and when taken, are made on the engrossed bill.

When the two Houses reach a complete agreement on all the amendments, the papers are delivered to the Enrolling Clerk of the House where the bill originated. The Enrolling Clerk prepares a copy of the bill in the form as finally agreed upon by the two Houses and sends it to the Government Printing Office for "enrollment," which means historically "written on parchment." The original papers on the bill are retained in the files of the originating House until the end of a Congress, when they are sent to the National Archives.

20

SIGNATURES OF SPEAKER AND VICE PRESIDENT

Upon receipt of an enrolled bill from the Government Printing Office, either the Secretary of the Senate or the Clerk of the House endorses it, certifying where the bill originated. If, after examination by the Enrolling Clerk of that House, the bill is found to be in the form agreed upon by both Houses, a slip is attached thereto stating that the bill, identified by number and title, has been examined and found truly enrolled. It is then presented to the Speaker of the House for his signature, which is announced in open session. Usually, enrolled bills are signed first by the Speaker. The bill is then transmitted by messenger to the Senate, where it is signed by the Vice President.

Under the rules of the House, the Committee on House Oversight is charged, when an enrolled bill has been duly signed by the Speaker and the Vice President, to present the same, when the bill has originated in the House, to the President of the United States for his signature "and report the fact and date of such presentation to the House." If it is a Senate bill, this responsibility of presenting the bill to the President falls on the Secretary of the Senate.

An error discovered in a bill after the legislative steps in its passage have been completed may be corrected by authority of a concurrent resolution, provided the bill has not yet been approved by the President. If the bill has not been enrolled, the error may be corrected in the enrollment; if it has been enrolled and signed by the Presiding Officers of the two Houses, or by the Speaker, such action may be rescinded by a concurrent resolution agreed to by the two Houses, and the bill correctly re-enrolled. If it has been presented to the President, but not acted upon by him, he may be requested by a concurrent resolution to return it to the Senate or the House for correction. If, however, the President has approved the bill, and it has thereby become a law, any amendment thereof can only be made by the passage of another bill, which must take the same course as the original.

21

PRESIDENTIAL ACTION: APPROVAL OR VETO

The President, under the Constitution, has 10 days (Sundays excepted) after the bill has been presented to him in which to act upon it. If the subject matter of the bill is within the jurisdiction of a department of the Government, or affects its interests in any way, he may in the meantime, at his discretion, refer the bill to the head of that department for investigation and a report thereon. The report of such official may serve as an aid to the President in reaching a decision about whether or not to approve the bill. If the President does approve it, he signs the bill, giving the date, and transmits this information by messenger to the Senate or the House, as the case might be. In the case of revenue and tariff bills, the hour of approval is usually indicated. The enrolled bill is delivered to the Archivist of the United States, who designates it as a public or private law, depending upon its purpose, and gives it a number. Public and private laws are numbered separately and serially. An official copy is sent to Government Printing Office to be used in making the so-called slip law print.

In the event the President does not desire to approve a bill, but is unwilling to veto it, he may, by not returning it within the 10-day period after it is presented to him, permit it to become a law without his approval. The Archivist makes an endorsement on the bill that, having been presented to the President of the United States for his approval and not having been returned to the House of Congress in which it originated within the time prescribed by the Constitution, it has become a law without his approval.

Where the 10-day period extends beyond the date of the final adjournment of Congress, the President may, within that time approve and sign the bill, which thereby becomes a law. If, however, in such a case, the President does not approve and sign the bill before the expiration of the ten-day period, it fails to become a law. This is what is known as a pocket veto. The United States Court of Appeals, in the case of *Kennedy v. Sampson*, 511 F.2d 430 (D.C. Cir., 1974), held that a Senate bill could not be pocket-vetoed by the President during an "intrasession" adjournment of Congress to a day certain for more than three days, where the Secretary of the Senate had been authorized to receive Presidential messages during such adjournment. In the case of *Barnes v. Kline*, 759 F.2d 51 (D.C. Cir., 1985), the Court held the same with regard to an intersession adjournment.

If the President does not favor a bill and vetoes it, he returns it to the House of origin without his approval, together with his objections thereto (referred to as the "veto message"). It should be noted that after the final adjournment of the 94th Congress, 1st session, the President returned two bills, giving Congress the opportunity to reconsider and "override" the vetoes.

The constitutional provision for reconsideration by the Senate is met, under the precedents, by the reading of the veto message, spreading it on the Journal, and adopting a motion (1) to act on it immediately, (2) to refer it, with the accompanying papers, to a standing committee: (3) to order that it lie on the table, to be subsequently considered, or (4) to order its consideration postponed to a definite day. The House's procedures are much the same.

If, upon reconsideration by either House, the House of origin acting first, the bill does not receive a two-thirds vote, the President's veto is sustained and the bill fails to become a law.

If a bill which has been vetoed is passed upon reconsideration by the first House by the required two-thirds vote, an endorsement to this effect is made on the back of the bill, and it is then transmitted, together with the accompanying message, to the second House for its action thereon. If likewise reconsidered and passed by that body, a similar endorsement is made thereon. The bill, which has thereby been enacted into law, is not again presented to the President, but is delivered to the Administrator of the General Services Administration for deposit in the Archives, and is printed, together with the attestations of the Secretary of the Senate and the Clerk of the House of its passage over the President's veto.

22

THE CONGRESSIONAL BUDGET PROCESS

The Congressional Budget and Impoundment Control Act was enacted in 1974 as a means for Congress to establish national budget priorities and the appropriate level of total revenues, expenditures, and debt for each year. Moreover, it provided for strict time limits in dealing with Presidential attempts to impound funds already appropriated either through deferrals or rescissions.

The Act has been amended so as to curb the practice of imposing unfunded Federal mandates on States and local governments, as well as to give the President line item veto authority with respect to appropriations, new direct spending, and limited tax benefits. There has also been added to the statutes a provision allowing the two

Houses of Congress to vote in an expeditious manner to reject rules issued by executive agencies.

Congress acts on a concurrent resolution on the budget in the spring of each year. This resolution sets levels of new budget authority and spending, revenue, and debt levels. However, Congress may adopt a later budget resolution that revises or reaffirms the most recently adopted budget resolution.

One of the mechanisms Congress uses to enforce projected budget authority and spending, revenue, and debt levels is called the reconciliation process. Under reconciliation, Congress in a budget resolution directs one or more legislative committees to report bills or recommend changes in laws that will achieve the levels of spending and revenues set by the budget resolution. The directions to the committees specify the total amounts that must be changed but leave to the discretion of the committees' decisions about the changes that must be made to achieve the required levels.

If only one committee has been directed to recommend changes, that committee reports its reconciliation legislation directly to the floor for consideration. If, however, more than one committee has been directed to make changes, the committees report the recommended changes to the Committee on the Budget. That committee then reports an omnibus reconciliation bill to the floor for consideration by the whole Senate or House.

23

EXECUTIVE BUSINESS AND EXECUTIVE SESSIONS

EXECUTIVE MATTERS GENERALLY

The executive business of the Senate consists of nominations and treaties submitted to the Senate by the President of the United States for its "advice and consent." This business of the Senate is handled separately from its legislative business.

Treaties are referred to the Committee on Foreign Relations. Nominations are referred to one of the various committees of the Senate; usually this is the committee that handled the legislation creating the position. When committees report treaties or nominations to the Senate, they are placed on the Executive Calendar, as distinct from the Calendar of Business, on which legislation is placed. These two calendars are printed separately.

When the Senate considers nominations and treaties, it goes into executive session, as distinct from legislative session, and a separate Journal is kept of the proceedings thereon.

NOMINATIONS

The scope of the Senate's authority to confirm Presidential nominations is vast. It includes officers of the Government—specifically, ambassadors, other public ministers and counsels, justices of the Supreme Court, all other officers of the United States as set forth in the Constitution, and such officers as Congress by law may designate.

A Presidential nomination requiring advice and consent must be approved by a majority vote of the Senate. After a nomination is received and referred to the appropriate committee, hearings may be held, and after the committee votes, the nomination may be reported back to the Senate. If the nomination is confirmed, a Resolution of Confirmation is transmitted to the White House and the appointment is then signed by the President.

Presidential nominations may be made during recesses of the Senate. The Constitution authorizes the President to "fill up" vacancies that may happen during such recesses "by granting Commissions which shall expire at the End of their next Session." Recess appointments to the Supreme Court, however, troubled the Senate enough that it agreed to a sense of the Senate resolution on August 29, 1960, stating that such appointments "may not be wholly consistent with the best interests of the Supreme Court, the nominee who may be involved, the litigants before the Court, nor indeed the people of the United States." It further stated "that such appointments, therefore, should not be made except under unusual circumstances and for the purpose of preventing or ending a demonstrable breakdown in the administration of the Court's business."

TREATIES

All confidential communications made by the President shall be kept secret, and all treaties which may be laid before the Senate, and all remarks, votes and proceedings thereon, shall also be kept secret until the Senate shall, by their resolution, take off the injunction of secrecy. When the Senate is proceeding on treaty ratification, the treaty shall be read a first time. Only a motion to refer it to committee, to print it in confidence for the use of the Senate, or to remove the injunction of secrecy shall be in order.

The rules for the consideration for executive business are different from the rules for the consideration and disposition of legislative business. Rule XXX provides that a treaty shall lie over for one day before the Senate proceeds to consider it in executive session; then it may be read a second time, after which amendments may be proposed. At any stage of these proceedings the Senate may remove the injunction of secrecy from the treaty. When there is no further debate or amendment to be proposed to the treaty, the Senate proceeds to consider a resolution of ratification.

After the resolution of ratification has been proposed, no amendment to the treaty is in order except by unanimous consent. On the other hand, reservations, etc., are in order only during consideration of the resolution of ratification, not while the treaty itself is being considered for amendment. After the Senate completes considering both the treaty and the resolution of ratification, it gives its final consent to the resolution by a two-thirds vote of the Senators present. The vote on a motion to postpone indefinitely requires the same two-thirds majority; all other motions and questions arising in relation to a treaty are decided by a majority vote.

AMENDMENTS, RESERVATIONS, AND OTHER STATEMENTS

The Senate may stipulate conditions to a treaty in the form of amendments, reservations, understandings, declarations, statements, interpretations, and statements in committee reports. An "amendment" makes actual changes in the language of the treaty.

The term "reservation" in treaty-making, according to general international usage, means a formal declaration by a state, when signing, ratifying, of adhering to a treaty, which modifies or limits the substantive effect of one or more of the treaty's provisions as between the reserving state and other states party to the treaty. In addition, the Senate may attach to resolutions of ratification various "understandings," "interpretations," "declarations," and so on. The term "understanding" is often used to designate a statement that is not intended to modify or limit any of the provisions of the treaty in its international operation, but instead is intended merely to clarify or explain the meaning of the treaty or to deal with some matter incidental to the operation of the treaty without constituting a substantive reservation. Any such additions to the resolution are part of the instrument of ratification no matter what they are called, and even if their effect is solely of an internal domestic nature.

RATIFICATION OF TREATIES

The word "ratification" when used in connection with treaties refers to the formal act by which a nation affirms its willingness to be bound by a specific international agreement. The basic purpose of ratification of a treaty is to confirm that an agreement which two or more countries have negotiated and signed is accepted and recognized as binding by those countries.

The procedure by which nations ratify treaties is a concern of domestic rather than international law. The Constitution does not use the word ratification in regard to treaties. It says only that the President shall have the power, by and with the advice and consent of the Senate, to make treaties. The Constitution does not divide up the process into various component parts which can be identified today, such as initiation, negotiation, signing, Senatorial advice and consent, ratification, deposit or exchange of the instruments of ratification, and promulgation. From the beginning, however, the formal act of ratification has been performed by the President acting "by and with the advice and consent of the Senate." The President ratifies the treaty, but only upon the authorization of the Senate.

The Senate gives its advice and consent by agreeing to the resolution of ratification. After it does so, the President is not obligated to proceed with the process of ratification. With the President's approval, however, the ratification occurs with the exchange of the instruments of ratification between the parties to the treaty.

Treaties, unlike any other business considered by the Senate, stay before that body once the President submits them until the Senate acts on them or unless the President requests, and/or the Senate adopts an order or resolution authorizing, their return to the President or the Secretary of State. In 1937, 1947, and 1952, the Senate returned numerous treaties, including some dating back as early as 1910, to the Secretary of State or the President.